Best-Ever Circle Time Activities: LANGUAGE BUILDING

50 Instant & Irresistible Activities & Games
That Build Phonemic Awareness, Expand Vocabulary,
and Strengthen Listening Skills

by Ellen Booth Church

New York • Toronto • London • Auckland • Sydney
Mexico City • New Delhi • Hong Kong • Buenos Aires **Teaching** *Resources*

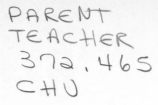

To my former co-teacher, Mary McLaughlin,
who taught me to love circle time instead of fear it!
Your creative and playful inspiration is at the heart of all I do.

Cover design by Maria Lilja
Cover illustration by Anne Kennedy
Interior design by Solutions by Design, Inc.
Interior illustration by James Hale

ISBN: 0-439-43113-1

Contents

Welcome!

Circle time is a language laboratory. In fact, it can be one of the most literacy-rich parts of the day! It is a time when children can experiment with all the elements of language as they read and write in a relaxed and playful atmosphere.

With the support of their circle time community around them, children venture into new linguistic territories. They hear new words and learn how to use them in context. They experience the fun of playing with words, sounds, and letters—and the joy of stories and books. They use higher-order critical thinking skills. They can even begin to develop writing skills!

Reading, writing, speaking, and listening are all communication skills—and what better place than circle time to communicate? Here you have the time and place for children to talk in front of a group, share an idea or opinion, make up a silly word or rhyme, or share their own writing.

In these pages you'll find tons of ideas to create literate circle times. Enjoy the journey!

Building Language Skills at Circle Time

A helpful way to conceptualize literacy skills is to think about the people you consider literate. What makes them literate? Are they simply good readers and writers, or is there something more? Literate people speak well, discuss and share ideas, and express feelings and opinions easily. They "play" with words and ideas. Literate people are thinkers. When discussing any topic, they predict, hypothesize, make deductions, and brainstorm. They question what they read and hear, and form their own opinions. Literate people know how to use writing as a tool of communication and understand that writing is both purposeful and fun. Keep these aspects of literacy in mind as you create literate circle times for young children!

Literacy research has emphasized that talking and having fun with language—its sounds, rhymes, rhythms, and meaning—are essential to learning. Young children can only make sense of reading in terms of the meaning and language they have already internalized—and they do this mostly by engaging with others. So every time you gather children for circle time, you are helping them build a broad range of skills!

Language-Building Skills

Some of the skills you'll help develop and build upon with the activities in this book are:

Communication Skills
- Auditory discrimination
- Conversation
- Creative expression
- Descriptive language
- Expressive language
- Following directions
- Group discussion
- Labeling
- Listening
- Receptive language
- Sharing
- Singing
- Speaking
- Storytelling
- Vocabulary

Thinking Skills
- Analysis
- Brainstorming
- Classification
- Comparing and contrasting
- Comprehension
- Deduction
- Evaluation
- Inference
- Interpretation
- Observation
- Prediction
- Synthesis

Writing Skills
- Conventions of print
- Drawing
- Expository writing
- Fine-motor coordination
- Handwriting
- Journal writing
- Labeling
- Left-to-right progression
- Letter writing
- Name writing
- Picture-story writing
- Spelling

Reading Skills
- Book awareness
- Functional print
- Letter recognition
- Letter-sound recognition
- Making predictions
- Name recognition
- Phonemic awareness
- Phonics
- Picture-word association
- Print awareness
- Retelling
- Rhyming
- Segmentation
- Sequencing
- Sound blending
- Sound isolation
- Visual discrimination
- Word recognition

A Circle Time Checkup

Since circle time is something you do every day, you'll want to evaluate it periodically to see how it's working. Use these questions to assess your circle time.

What's Working?

- Do children seem excited to come to circle time and happy to be there?
- Do children seem relaxed and comfortable as well as attentive?
- Do children express their ideas?
- Do other children listen while one child is speaking?
- Do children seem to be developing a sense of community?
- Are *you* having a good time with the children?

What's Not Working?

- Do children resist coming to circle time?
- Do children seem restless or distracted?
- Do you find yourself frequently telling children to listen and quiet down?
- Are both you and the children eager for circle time to be over?
- Are one or two children monopolizing discussions?

Strategies for Improvement:

- Try a shorter circle time, or even taking a break from circle time for a while.
- Break into two smaller circles.
- Try adding a new and engaging ritual or song to begin and end circle time.
- Allow individual children who seem to struggle during circle time the option of another activity. Welcome them back to the circle when they are ready!
- Look to see if the circle happens at a good time of the morning. Children may need more independent playtime before coming together as a group.
- Vary the pace and content of your circle time activities.
- Balance active and passive activities.
- If things really aren't going well one day, don't sweat it! Find a positive way to end, move on to another activity, and try again the next day.

Introducing Functional Print at Circle Time

Functional print is any type of print or text that serves a function in everyday life. It is what people read most in their daily lives and is often taken for granted, yet it is a vital means of communication. Here are some suggestions for introducing functional print into the circle time area and beyond.

- ◉ Post daily notices relating to classroom life in the circle time area.

- ◉ Make labels, titles, captions for objects, pictures, and displays.

- ◉ Create a bookshelf of books created by children.

- ◉ Every day at circle time, use a calendar for marking time, birthdays, and special events.

- ◉ Use chart paper at circle time to record new words and ideas as they come up.

A Variety of Language-Building Circles

This book is divided into seven sections:

Talking Circles

Here you'll find circle time activities for developing language and starting great discussions. The first step in literacy development is oral language, and circle time is the perfect place for children to express themselves in a variety of ways. Talking in front of a group is sometimes challenging for young children—try some of these special games to spark the speaker within every child.

Story Circles

In this section, you'll find games and activities that help children develop critical-thinking skills related to stories and books. Stories can be magical doorways to playful interaction—and all the while, children are practicing inference, deduction, comparison, analysis, and evaluation. These skills lay the foundation for literacy. Try these activities, and encourage your group to be literate thinkers!

Word Circles

This section is full of playful ways to build vocabulary. Circle time is a vocabulary-rich "Crock-Pot" of creative linguistic experiences. It is the perfect place to introduce new words, to use them in songs and games, to expand understanding of words, and even to make up new ones. Mix all the ingredients together with a healthy helping of fun, and you have the ideal recipe for vocabulary development.

Phonics Circles

This section is filled with circle time activities for exploring phonemes, syllables, and blends. The world is full of wonderful things to hear and listen to. Young children are developing the auditory perception and discrimination skills essential to learning how to read and write.

Writing Circles

Children learn by observing writing as well as writing themselves. This section provides you with a variety of circle time activities to introduce the writing process through modeling and participation. Together, you and your class will experiment with creative and expository writing in easy, cooperative activities. Filled with everything from story writing to list making, this section is a hands-on primer in the writing process.

Question Circles

These activities will help you ask great questions and invite children to put their literacy skills to use. Do you ever "wonder out loud"? It can be one of the greatest tools you can use to stimulate curiosity and creativity in your circle time gathering. The best way to spark children's discussions is to ask questions. With good questions, you get good conversations—the core of language and literacy development!

Alphabet Circles

Here you'll find songs, games, and activities for learning the alphabet. Recognizing, forming, matching, saying, and hearing letters are core skills in learning how to read and write. Learning the alphabet can be all fun and games with these easy circle time activities!

Here's what you'll find on each page:

Materials List

Many of the activities in this book require no materials at all; when they do, they're listed here.

Skills

This list tells you which skills you're developing during your circle time.

How-To

Simple step-by-step instructions let you know how to make the activity happen.

Songs and Rhymes

Often a song sung to a familiar tune is included. You can copy it onto sentence strips and use a pocket chart to teach children the song, or simply sing it through several times until children are familiar with it.

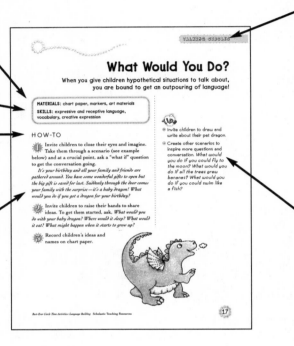

Section

Look here to check the area of language development upon which the activity focuses.

Tips

You'll find plenty of ways to simplify, extend, or enrich the activity.

Terrific Tips for Successful Circle Times

◉ **Start with short circle times.** Leave them wanting more!

◉ **Don't require attendance,** but be so interesting that children just *have* to come over to see what is going on!

◉ **Keep a balance** of active participation and passive listening. If children are losing interest, do something active.

◉ **Exaggerate positive behaviors** you want to reinforce. Make a point of using *please* and *thank you*. Look at the child who is talking instead of the child who is interrupting and say, *I am listening to Jerome now.*

◉ **Respond proactively to behavior problems.** Seat children who have trouble focusing next to good listeners or your aide. Before circle time, talk to the child about your expectations for behavior and reinforce his or her ability to meet them.

◉ **Make eye contact** with children. Your eyes are probably the strongest management tool you have!

◉ **Practice, practice, practice** whatever you want to do with children before you come to circle time. This will allow you to be relaxed and to have close contact with children, rather than focusing solely on the materials.

◉ **Be ready to go.** Collect all materials before children arrive (waiting time creates chaos!).

◉ **Encourage children to talk.** Be sure you're not talking more than they are.

◉ **Acknowledge the rights of every member** of the group.

◉ **Use a consistent place and time** so that children know what to expect.

◉ **Be flexible.** If children are not "with you," then it is time to end the session. Find a positive ending and closure for the group.

◉ **Use clear and simple directions** so that children know what you expect of them at circle time.

◉ **Be dramatic,** change your voice, whisper, make obvious mistakes, use riddles, be humorous, but most of all…involve children.

◉ **Ask open-ended questions.** *What would happen if____? What do you think about ____? What do you imagine? How many ways can you ____?*

◉ **Watch for "invisible" or isolated children.** They will need your extra attention at circle time. Be sure to deliberately involve them as much as possible.

◉ **If all else fails, read a good book.** Literature captivates children in ways that nothing else can.

Tell and Show

Take this age-old circle time activity and update it by reversing the game—and adding a song!

HOW-TO

1 In advance, designate a "child of the day." Send home a letter inviting that child to choose an object from home to share with the group. Hide the object in the bag.

2 Introduce the child of the day. Write the child's name at the top of a sheet of chart paper. Say, for instance, *Sarah has a surprise in her bag that she is going to tell us about. Our job is to ask questions and try to guess what it is.*

3 Sing a song to get the activity started:

Tell, Tell, Tell Us Please
(Tune: "Row, Row Your Boat")

Tell, tell, tell us please,
What's hiding in your bag?
Tell us please, oh tell us please,
What's hiding in your bag?
Give, give, give a clue,
What's hiding in your bag?
Listen friends and figure out
What's hiding in the bag.

The child with the bag then gives one-sentence clues. For instance, if the object is a teddy bear, the child might say, *It is soft. I sleep with it.* You might help children get started: *What color is it? What shape is it? What do you do with it?*

4 Invite the child of the day to pass the closed bag around so that children may feel the object and continue to guess. Finally, have the child of the day open the bag and show the group what's inside.

MATERIALS: pillowcase or shopping bag, chart paper, marker

SKILLS: expressive language, vocabulary, group discussion, singing

- Ask families to help children think of clues for their hidden object before they bring it to school. Suggest that they write the clues on an index card for the child to bring to school.

- If the designated child of the day forgets his or her object at home, simply invite him or her to choose something special from the classroom.

Talk With Me!

Sometimes it's difficult to get children to speak at circle time. By giving interesting sentence starters, you get them not only talking but also listening to each other!

HOW-TO

1 Explain that today you are going to play a talking game with the group: *I am going to say the beginning of a sentence and each of you can finish. The sentence today is "I was very happy when..."*

2 Invite children to take turns finishing the sentence. As each child shares, be sure all children are listening to the speaker. Make a point of looking at the child who is speaking, and direct children's attention toward that child.

3 After a child has shared about a time he or she was very happy, ask the group, *Who can remember what [child's name] said about the time he or she was very happy? Can you tell us what you remember?* Invite the original speaker to confirm if that was what he or she said.

4 Now move to the next child who is interested in sharing. Offer the sentence starter again to get things going. Repeat until all children who want a turn have had one.

MATERIALS: none

SKILLS: speaking, group discussion, vocabulary, listening, sharing

- Children can later illustrate their idea at the writing center. They can dictate the story to an adult.

- Other sentence starters include: *I was sad once when..., I was excited when I found out..., My favorite thing to do is..., My favorite holiday is...*

Tell Me a Drawing

Children will have fun telling you what to do as they use vocabulary and descriptive language to "paint a picture."

HOW-TO

1 Say, *I have a problem that you may be able to help me with. I want to draw a picture of a dog but I can't remember how. Can you tell me what to draw?*

2 Put your marker on the page and ask, *What should I draw first? Can you name one part of a dog?* Draw whatever part they suggest.

Add a song to the fun!

> **This Old Dog**
> (Tune: "This Old Man")
>
> *This old dog, here's his_____[head]_____,*
>   (children fill in body part)
> *He played knick knack on my ___[bed]_____,*
>   (add rhyming word)
> *With a knick knack paddy whack, draw another part,*
> *This old dog is really smart!*

3 Ask, *Does it look like a dog now? What else should I draw to make a dog?* Sing the song and add parts until the dog is complete.

MATERIALS: drawing or chart paper, markers and crayons

SKILLS: expressive and descriptive language, singing, vocabulary, labeling

- Remember, you don't have to be an artist to draw for children. Most children think you are a wonderful artist no matter how well you draw!

- Ask children to suggest other things they would like to help you draw (a house, car, face, and so on).

- Having children help you draw something from your current theme (such as dinosaurs or transportation) is an excellent assessment tool. If they can verbalize how to draw something, they know a great deal about it!

Interview Favorites

Help children structure their conversations with each other. In this activity, children practice talking to each other in a structured interview format.

HOW-TO

1 In advance, create an interview sheet on chart paper. Tell children they are going to be discussing their very favorite things. Write a word and draw a corresponding picture for each interview topic, such as *ice cream* (with a picture of an ice cream cone), *book* (with a picture of a book), sport, shape, song, and TV show.

2 Have children turn to the child seated next to them. Explain, *One partner in each pair will start. You will interview your friends as if you were on television. This sheet will help you ask your friend about his or her favorite things. Look at the picture at the top. Which favorite thing will you ask about?* Demonstrate to help get children started.

3 After a few minutes, have children switch roles and interview the other partner. Then go around the circle and invite children to tell about one thing they remember as their partner's favorite!

MATERIALS: chart paper, marker

SKILLS: expressive and receptive language, conversation, picture-word association, vocabulary

- Let children take turns using a tape recorder. Later, put the tapes in the listening center for children to listen to.

- On chart paper, create a bar graph of the interviews. Choose one of the favorites, such as color, and have children come up and "vote" for their choice.

What Would You Do?

When you give children hypothetical situations to talk about, you are bound to get an outpouring of language!

MATERIALS: chart paper, marker

SKILLS: expressive and receptive language, vocabulary, creative expression

HOW-TO

 Invite children to close their eyes and imagine. Take them through a scenario (see example below) and at a crucial point, ask a "what if" question to get the conversation going.

It's your birthday and all your family and friends are gathered around. You have some wonderful gifts to open but the big gift is saved for last. Suddenly, through the door comes your family with the surprise—it's a baby dragon! What would you do if you got a dragon for your birthday?

2 Invite children to raise their hands to share ideas. To get them started, ask, *What would you do with your baby dragon? Where would it sleep? What would it eat? What might happen when it starts to grow up?*

3 Record children's ideas and names on chart paper.

- Invite children to draw and write about their pet dragon.

- Create other scenarios to inspire more questions and conversation. *What would you do if you could fly to the moon? What would you do if bananas grew from all trees? What would you do if you could swim like a fish?*

Use Your Words!

There are many wonderful books with great illustrations and no words. Use them to get children talking—and start them on the road to storytelling.

HOW-TO

1 Show children the picture book and ask, *Where is the story in this book? What part do I read?* Children may notice that there are no words in the book and that the pictures tell a story.

2 Show the cover of the book and invite children to suggest how to open it and turn the pages. You can even pretend to start the book upside down or from the back as a way to get them involved. They will quickly tell you you're wrong!

3 Slowly turn the pages from left to right, taking time to show the pictures. Don't try to tell the story; just ask children to look at the pictures quietly as you turn.

4 At the end, ask, *What do you think the book was about? What did the pictures tell you about the story?* Invite any and all interpretations of the silent story.

5 Say, *Now it is time to use your words. I am going to turn the pages and you can tell the story from the pictures!* As you turn the pages slowly, children can take turns telling a story. You can ask questions to help them get started. *Who or what is the story about? What happens on this page?*

MATERIALS: wordless picture books, such as *Rain*, by Peter Spier (Doubleday, 1982), or the *The Snowman*, by Raymond Briggs (Random House, 1978)

SKILLS: expressive language, left-to-right progression, creative expression

- Enjoy the story several times. You will probably get different stories each time children "use their words."

- Encourage children to make their own wordless books. Every picture tells a story!

What's My Job?

Have you ever had a talkative child suddenly clam up when there's a visitor? Here is a fun game that will get children asking questions and talking!

HOW-TO

1 Arrange for someone with an interesting job to visit. Invite him or her to bring props or pictures to help children identify what they do.

2 Prepare children for the surprise guest. Explain that someone who does a special job is coming to visit circle time and *their* job will be to ask questions that help them guess what the guest's job is! On the day of the visit, display chart paper in the circle time area (write "What's My Job?" at the top) and set out a special chair for the visitor.

3 Gather children around the chair and usher the visitor in with great gusto and drama. Together, sing:

> **Can You Tell Us What You Do?**
> (Tune: "London Bridge")
>
> *Can you tell us what you do?*
> *What you do? What you do?*
> *Can you give a tiny clue?*
> *Our new visitor!*

4 Have the visitor show a prop as a clue (start with one that is general to keep children guessing and talking for a while). Ask children to suggest what the object is used for. Record their ideas.

5 Ask the visitor to keep sharing props or giving clues to help the guessing game continue. After several rounds, have children guess the visitor's job!

MATERIALS: chart paper, marker

SKILLS: expressive language, conversation, singing, group discussion

Tips

● Afterward, ask the visitor to stay in the circle time area to provide small group conversations and hands-on experiences with children.

● Afterward, write a thank-you letter from the class, thanking the visitor for coming.

Book Detectives

Children often use a book's cover to help them interpret the story. This is inference: the use of different pieces of evidence to draw a conclusion.

HOW-TO

1. Introduce a new picture book by placing the "spy hole" over the cover to reveal only part of it. Say a little chant to get the game going:

   Look through the circle and what do you see?
   A part of the book, looking at me!
   Move the circle and what do you see?
   More that tells what the story will be!

2. Move the cardboard around to show different parts of the book. This will encourage children to collect more evidence. Ask, *What do you notice now? What does this clue tell you about the story?*

3. Write children's clues on chart paper as they describe what they see. Accept all suggestions.

4. After a while, show the cover to see how accurately they guessed. Children enjoy using the cardboard spy hole on pages inside the book, too.

MATERIALS: various picture books (ones children haven't seen yet), piece of cardboard (larger than the book covers with a round "spy hole" cut in it), chart paper, marker

SKILLS: observation, visual discrimination, group discussion, expressive and descriptive language, inference

Tips

- Start with a book with a familiar character, such as Clifford or Franklin. Children can easily guess who is in the book.

- This activity can continue long after group time is over. Children enjoy exploring books on their own in the library area, using the cardboard spy hole.

- To work on letter recognition, write a large letter on chart paper. Then cover parts of it and ask children to figure out what it is!

Buddy-Up With a Book

Have you ever watched a young child "read" a book by its pictures? In this activity, children share the joy of their own inventive reading with a partner!

HOW-TO

1. Before circle time, ask children to find one of their favorite books to bring to the circle.

2. Explain that today, instead of having you read a story to the group, they are all going to get to "read" a story to a friend: *You and the person sitting next to you will take turns reading your favorite story to each other.* Have children in the circle scoot back a bit so they can focus on their reading and listening.

3. Explain to children that they don't have to be able to read all the words, but that they can tell the story in their own way, using the pictures and what they remember about the story. Provide plenty of time for children to "read" their stories to each other. Remind children to start with the cover and turn the pages from the front cover to the back of the book and read from left to right. Wander around the group as children read, and assist them if necessary.

4. Ring a bell or chime when the second child should start reading. At the end, ring it again to notify children it is time to stop.

MATERIALS: favorite storybooks, bell

SKILLS: book awareness, print awareness, left-to-right progression, storytelling, sequencing

- Children can also bring favorites from home for Buddy-Up reading time.

- Invite a child to read his or her book to the entire group.

Storytime Sleuth

Young children love to use clues to solve a mystery. Being able to deduce—conclude by logical reasoning—is invaluable for the development of reading comprehension skills.

> **MATERIALS:** favorite stories, pillowcase or drawstring bag, chart paper, markers
>
> **SKILLS:** listening, expressive language, group discussion, deduction

HOW-TO

1 Give children verbal clues they can combine to guess the story you are going to read (put the book in a pillowcase or bag before beginning). It is best to use familiar stories and books with favorite characters. For instance, if using a Clifford book, you might say, *I am thinking of a character from several of our favorite books that likes to help others. He is an animal.*

2 As children suggest different characters they know, write them on chart paper. Add another clue. For instance, if using a Clifford book, say, *This character is also very big.* Then ask children to look at the chart to see if any of the characters are big, and cross off all those that are not.

3 Next, give children another clue, such as *This character is also red and barks.* Invite children to guess the character. When they guess correctly, write the character's name on the chart so that children can see the name in print. Then read the book to celebrate!

Tips

● Give clues for favorite fairy tales: *Which story has someone who likes to eat and sleep at someone else's house? Someone who has blond hair?* (Goldilocks!)

● Try using nursery rhymes, too! Ask, *Which rhyme is about a mother with lots of children?* (There was an Old Woman Who Lived in a Shoe) *Which rhyme is about an egg?* (Humpty Dumpty)

● Eventually, children will be able to give clues for books and stories themselves. Provide a storytime sleuth hat or magnifying glass that children can use for dramatic effect!

Your Opinion Counts!

Young children can have strong opinions about stories and books. When children state their opinions, they are using their evaluation skills—the ability to interpret and judge story elements and characterization.

HOW-TO

1 Choose a book with a "meaty" story about which children might have strong opinions. Invite children to evaluate how a character handled a situation or the outcome of the story. For instance, after reading or telling the story of Three Billy Goats Gruff, ask, *Which character do you think was the smartest? If you were in the story, would you rather be the troll or one of the goats? Why?* By asking specific questions, you involve children with the content of the story and help them to base their overall evaluation on critical thinking as well as their feelings. Then ask, *Did you like the story? What did you like about it? What didn't you like?*

2 Ask, *How could you improve the story? What would you change or add to make the story better?* This will give children an active experience with the author's craft.

3 Write children's names and their comments on chart paper. Over time you can create a "book review" list in the circle time area. Children can choose their favorites from categories such as Great Characters, Exciting Stories, Scary Stories, Beautiful Illustrations—whatever *they* choose as important elements to review.

MATERIALS: books, chart paper, marker

SKILLS: observation, expressive language, group discussion, evaluation

● Print a class book review and send it home to families. Not only will families love reading what their children had to say, but they can also use the list to inform book choices at home!

Fact or Fantasy?

Preschool and kindergarten children are beginning to notice the difference between fantasy and reality in books and stories. In doing so, they are using the critical-thinking skills of analysis and comparison.

HOW-TO

1 Invite children to collect books about animals from the class library (and from home). Ask, *How many books about animals can we find? Let's go on a treasure hunt to see!*

2 Explain the terms *fantasy* and *fact*: *Stories that are fantasy are pretend and those that are fact are about real things.* You might illustrate this with a book from the Franklin series, in which animals speak or wear clothing. Then show a book about real turtles.

3 Ask children to examine the collected books and decide if the books are fact or fantasy. Ask: *How do we know? What kind of clues indicate that a book is about a pretend animal?* Children can look for clues that suggest it is a fantasy, such as animals wearing clothes or doing other human activities.

4 Choose one fact book and one fantasy book as models, and have children sort the rest of the books into two piles, one fact and one fantasy.

MATERIALS: fiction and nonfiction books about animals

SKILLS: observation, expressive language, group discussion, analysis, comparing and contrasting

TIPS

- Eventually, move on to stories about people. These are more challenging for children to categorize as fact or fantasy!

- Invite children to choose an animal and create both a fiction and nonfiction book about it. Ask: *How are the stories different? How are they the same?*

Sensational Sequels

Children can combine critical- and creative-thinking skills by creating fun, silly sequels to their favorite stories and nursery rhymes.

MATERIALS: chart paper, marker

SKILLS: expressive language, evaluation, synthesis, comprehension, creative expression

HOW-TO

 1 Write a familiar nursery rhyme, such as Jack and Jill, on chart paper. Read it together and talk about it, asking comprehension questions, such as *What happened to Jack and Jill in the rhyme?*

2 After children have discussed what actually happened in the rhyme, ask them to consider what might happen next: *What if there was another verse that told what happened next? What would it say?* Try questions such as *What happened after Jack and Jill fell down? What did Mary do when her lamb followed her to school? What could Old Mother Hubbard do to feed her dog? Tell what happened next.*

3 Record children's sequels on chart paper (they need not rhyme).

⊙ After children suggest sequels for nursery rhymes, they can move on to more in-depth stories. Try familiar fairy tales next, and eventually have children suggest sequels for books they love.

Jack and Jill
Part 2:
Then Jill got up.
She helped Jack to get up.
They went to the nurse.

Create Your Own Ending

Invite children to create a conclusion for a story.
They will be using the critical skills of deduction and analysis.

MATERIALS: book with an exciting story line, such as *Cloudy With a Chance of Meatballs,* by Judi Barrett (Aladdin, 1982), chart paper, marker

SKILLS: comprehension, evaluation, deduction, analysis, group discussion

HOW-TO

 Read aloud *Cloudy With a Chance of Meatballs.* In the story, the town of Chewandswallow is covered in food and the people have to escape. Stop reading the book at this point and invite children to suggest what they would do to solve the problem. Ask: *How would you get away from town? Where would you go? What would you do when you got there?*

 Record children's ideas on chart paper, along with their names.

 Finish by reading the real ending to the book!

- Try this with other books—or even a video version of a favorite story.

- For an extra challenge for older children, read the end of a story and have children speculate about the beginning.

Wordy Brainstorms

Help children build new vocabulary and deepen their understanding of the current theme unit with a simple brainstorming activity.

> **MATERIALS:** chart paper, marker
>
> **SKILLS:** vocabulary, expressive language, brainstorming, classification

HOW-TO

 Write a word for a category of things related to your current theme. For instance, if focusing on transportation, write "vehicles" on chart paper.

 Start the brainstorming with a question: *How many different "things that go," or vehicles, can you think of? What would be something that moves or takes people on the go?*

3 As each child suggests a word, write it on the chart paper.

4 Find out how much children know about the words they are suggesting. Ask, *How do you know this is a vehicle? What makes it go? Who uses it?*

5 Keep the list up in the writing center so that children can use the words in their writing.

● Try this game with any theme (zoo, farm, pets, foods, plants, underwater life, insects, dinosaurs, and so on). This activity inspires vocabulary development and accesses children's prior knowledge.

Things That Grow
plants
animals
babies
fingernails
grass
hair
kittens

I'm Thinking of a Word

What happens when you reverse brainstorming?
You get a guessing game that builds vocabulary!

HOW-TO

1 In advance, write a noun on chart paper and cover it with dark paper. You might use a word related to a theme, such as weather or season words, names of animals, or types of jobs.

2 Ask children to join you in a guessing game. *I have a mystery word written here. I am going to give you clues to help you guess what it is!*

3 Give word clues. For instance, if the mystery word is *rain*, give words such as *water, drop, puddle,* and *umbrella.* Use a song to share your clues:

> **I'm Thinking of a Word**
> (Tune: "Farmer in the Dell")
>
> *I'm thinking of a word,*
> *I'm thinking of a word.*
> *Hi-Ho, what can it be?*
> *I'm thinking of a word.*
> *The clue word is WATER,*
> *The clue word is WATER.*
> *Hi-Ho, what can it be?*
> *The clue word is WATER.*

4 Write the clue words on chart paper and add a simple drawing to illustrate each. Then say, *Let's read all the words we have collected. Can you think of something that all these words describe?* Invite children to guess the word, then remove the dark paper to reveal.

MATERIALS: chart paper, marker, sheet of dark paper

SKILLS: vocabulary, word recognition, deduction, expressive language, singing

---

Tips

- The following day, invite children to use the mystery word and the clue words in a class story. Record it on chart paper as they dictate it to you.

- This is a great game to play with words related to different holidays! (*candy cane, shamrock, turkey,* and so on)

- Let one child be the leader, and have the class guess his or her mystery word.

One More Thing

This adjective game can go on, and on, and on.
In this game, children keep adding a word to describe
something—until there is a long list of words to remember!

MATERIALS: objects or pictures that inspire children to use descriptive words, chart paper, marker

SKILLS: receptive and expressive language, vocabulary, observation, classification

HOW-TO

1 Show children the object or picture and ask them to tell you what it is (for instance, a car). Then ask them to say "one more thing" about it (such as *It is yellow*). Write the following sentence on chart paper: "The car is yellow."

2 Ask children to keep adding words to describe it, and record adjectives and descriptive phrases as you go ("The car is yellow, shiny, with big windows, bumpy tires, round lights," and so on).

3 Put it all together. Ask, *Can you remember all the adjectives we used to describe this thing?* Read the sentence aloud together as you track the words with your finger.

● Reverse it! Record the descriptive words the group generated. Instead of showing the object or picture, read the descriptive words aloud and ask children to guess what the object was.

The Bear
is **brown**
has a **big** belly
has **pink** ears
has **shiny** eyes
is **fuzzy**

The Opposite Pokie

Build awareness of opposites while helping kids follow directions.
Here, children not only hear the words but move to them, too!

HOW-TO

1 Say, *I have a song today that you can sing and move to. But you have to listen carefully because the words keep changing.* Share the song:

> **The Opposite Pokie**
> (Tune: "Hokie Pokie")
>
> *You put your left foot **in**,*
> *You put your left foot **out**,*
> *You put your left foot **in**,*
> *And shake it all about.*
> *You do the hokie pokie*
> *And you wiggle **left** and **right**,*
> *That's what's out of sight!*
> *You put your right arm **up**,*
> *You put your right arm **down**,*
> *You put your right arm **up**,*
> *And shake it all about.*
> *You do the hokie pokie*
> *And you wiggle **left** and **right**,*
> *That's what's out of sight!*

2 With each verse, add different directions, such as *front* and *back*.

MATERIALS: none

SKILLS: receptive and expressive language, singing, vocabulary

- Use a prop such as a hoop, ball, or block to demonstrate the concept of opposites. Ask, *How can you show "on and off" with the block? Can you show "in and out" with the ball?*

- Each time you introduce a new pair of opposites, invite children to practice how they will show the word. Ask, *How will you show "right" and "left"?*

Nonsense Words

Playing with nonsense words is a great way for children to experiment with letter sounds, rhymes, and syllables.

MATERIALS: chart paper, marker

SKILLS: phonemic awareness, letter recognition, rhyming, singing

HOW-TO

 Write nonsense words such as *bibbily bobbily* on chart paper. Then write the alphabet down the left side of the paper. Sing the song:

> **Can You Say?**
> (Tune: "Ten Little Indians")
>
> *Can you say, Bibbily, bobbily?*
> *Can you say, Cibbily, cobbily?*
> *Can you say, Dibbily, dobbily?*
> *Sing it loud and clear!*
>
> (repeat the song using other consonant sounds)

2 Another time, try using different nonsense words, such as *bippity boppity* or *boogily bogily*.

● The format for the song can easily accommodate other nonsense words. Invite children to suggest some!

● Another great letter song that uses nonsense words is the classic "The Name Game." (*Ellen, Ellen, Bo Bellen, Banana Fana Fo Fellen, Fi Fie Mo Mellen, Ellen!*)

Charades

Pantomiming is a great way to build vocabulary.
In this game, children act out words for others to guess!

> **MATERIALS:** index cards, old magazines, glue, chart paper, markers
>
> **SKILLS:** receptive and expressive language, vocabulary, creative expression

HOW-TO

1 Using pictures cut from magazines, glue, and a marker, make picture-word cards. You might start with action words (picture of child running labeled "running," and so on).

2 Hand a card to the first player and have him or her act out the word. Ask, *How can you show us what your word is without saying it?*

3 First, demonstrate the process for children a few times. Eventually, you will have a circle of children calling out words!

4 When children guess the correct word, have the child who acted it out show the picture-word card to the group. Write the word on chart paper, asking children to help you spell it out, and then read it aloud together.

Tips

◉ As children become comfortable with the process, move from verbs to nouns (such as *dog, cat, train, toaster*).

◉ When children find an interesting new word, ask them to help you make a card for it and add it to the pantomime collection.

◉ Keep the pantomime cards in your circle time area and use them as a quick game during transitions.

The Dog on the Bus

Familiar songs such as "The Wheels on the Bus" can be used to introduce new words. By inviting children to add their own verses within the familiar structure of the song, you help expand vocabulary.

HOW-TO

1 Use a pillowcase or bag to store objects such as stuffed animals, a small ball, a bell, a doll, and so on. Sing the original "Wheels on the Bus" song together.

The Wheels on the Bus

The wheels on the bus go round and round,
Round and round, round and round.
The wheels on the bus go round and round,
All through the town.

Additional Verses:

The wipers on the bus go swish, swish, swish,
The horn on the bus goes beep, beep, beep,
The babies on the bus go waa, waa, waa,
The parents on the bus go shh, shh, shh,

2 After singing the original song together, invite children to suggest other things (silly as well as logical) that might be on the bus. Use the prop bag for inspiration. For instance, if you pull out a stuffed dog, ask, *What would the dog on the bus say?* Then sing the song together, using the new verse the children have created:

The dog on the bus goes arf, arf, arf,
Arf, arf, arf! Arf, arf, arf!
The dog on the bus goes arf, arf, arf,
All through the town!

3 Eventually, children will be able to suggest their own ideas of what could be happening on the bus—and sing a verse reflecting their ideas!

MATERIALS: pillow case or bag, small objects

SKILLS: vocabulary development, creative expression, phonemic awareness, singing

Tips

◉ Suggest other verses such as

The bell on the bus goes ting,
ting, ting,

The ball on the bus goes bounce, bounce, bounce,

The pizza on the bus gets eaten right up!

◉ Write children's suggested verses on chart paper for reference. They can read and sing the song again and again with their new verses.

◉ Provide mural paper with the outline of an empty giant bus in which children can draw pictures of all the crazy things they sang about!

The Missing Rhyme

Songs and rhyming are a natural combination! Encourage children to build rhyming skills by leaving off the last word of a phrase in a song.

> **MATERIALS:** chart paper, marker
>
> **SKILLS:** vocabulary development, phonemic awareness, rhyming, creative expression, listening, singing

HOW-TO

1 Take a familiar rhyming song such as "This Old Man" and sing it straight through with children.

2 Sing the song again, leaving off the rhyming word at the end of each phrase. *This old man, he played three. He played knick-knack on my _____.* Then ask, *How many different words can you think of that rhyme with* three? *Let's try them in the song, too!* Sing the song using children's ideas.

3 Sing again, expanding children's skills by asking them to suggest rhymes for the numbers 11 through 20! Remember that nonsense or made-up rhyming words are fine, because the idea is for children to hear the sound that matches. *What rhymes with twenty?* (plenty!)

 Tip

⊙ Use chart paper to write all the words children suggest. For instance, under the numeral 1, write all the words that rhyme (*sun, fun, ton*).

This old man, He played two, He played knick-knack on my shoe...

Body Bingo

The process of learning any song involves essential listening skills. You can use your favorite circle time songs as a tool for listening practice.

> **MATERIALS:** none
>
> **SKILLS:** listening, speaking, singing, vocabulary, sequencing, rhyming, creative expression

HOW-TO

1 Explain that this version of the song "Bingo" requires children to use their whole bodies. Children have to listen carefully and replace one letter of the word BINGO with a movement. Sing the song, substituting the letter *B* with a clap. Then ask children to try the verse themselves.

BINGO

There was a teacher had a dog,
And BINGO was his name-o.
B-I-N-G-O, B-I-N-G-O, B-I-N-G-O,
And BINGO was his name-o.
There was a teacher had a dog,
And BINGO was his name-o.
(clap)-I-N-G-O, (clap)-I-N-G-O, (clap)-I-N-G-O,
And BINGO was his name-o.

2 Continue, replacing each of the letters with a different movement:

B: clap
I: tap head
N: tap shoulders
G: pat belly
O: tap knees

Tips

- Try changing the name in the song to a child's name, and invite that child to make up movements to go with his or her name!

- Surprise children by singing a familiar song the wrong way (*The Farmer in the Well; Ring Around Their Toesies; Twinkle, Twinkle, Great Big Cat*). Invite them to join you in your silly song: *Twinkle, twinkle, great big cat, squished the pillow where he sat!*

Sing a Sound!

In this silly game, children get practice with phonemes by purposefully singing songs with letter sounds instead of words!

MATERIALS: none

SKILLS: phonemic awareness, sound isolation, singing

HOW-TO

1 Ask children if they have ever forgotten words to a song. *What do you do when you want to keep singing? Do you know you can use a sound instead of words?*

2 Tell children that they are going to sing songs with made-up sounds. For instance, *How would you sing "Twinkle, Twinkle, Little Star" with the sound of the letter M? Let's try it together.* Simply repeat the /m/ sound to the tune, without using any words.

3 Ask children to suggest a different letter sound to try with the same song.

4 Make it even harder and sillier! This time, invite children to sing the words to "Twinkle, Twinkle," but change their beginning sounds. *Let's all join in a round of Binkle, Binkle, Bittle Bar!* Repeat with different sounds.

Tips

⦿ Choose a new song and ask children to suggest a letter sound. Then you sing the song using the sound. Ask children to guess what song you are singing.

⦿ Try singing an entire song with just a letter sound. If you use M, it will sound like humming! Ask, *What other letter sounds are easy to sing?* (a, e, h, i, l, o, r, s, w, z)

Stretch It Out

Part of learning to read is the process of segmenting and sounding out words. Build this skill in a fun circle time activity.

> **MATERIALS:** five familiar objects such as a banana, block, ball, doll, crayon, and so on
>
> **SKILLS:** phonemic awareness, sound blending, segmentation

HOW-TO

1 Place a row of familiar objects on the floor. Explain that you are going to stretch the words out as you say them and children have to guess which object you are saying! *Bbbaaa-nnnaaa-nnnaaa. Which word did I say? Can you say the word the usual way? Banana! Let's say it together both the long and the short way.*

2 Choose another object in the row (without indicating to children which object you have chosen) and stretch out its name slowly for children to listen to and guess. When they have guessed correctly, hold up the object.

3 At the end of the game, excuse children from circle time by calling their names in an elongated way and ask children to guess who it is. *Listen carefully to who can be excused from circle. Berrrr-nnnna-det. Who is it? Bernadette.*

 Tips

- Eventually, introduce written words for children to segment and sound out. Start with words they have used in this game and move on to more unfamiliar words.

- Have a child lead the activity, stretching out a word and inviting the rest of the group to guess it.

Sir Rhymes-a-Lot

Young children love it when you say a funny word or sound. In this game you introduce Sir Rhymes-a-Lot, a puppet that makes up silly rhymes all the time!

HOW-TO

1 Introduce Sir Rhymes-a-Lot: *I have a new friend for you to meet. He is pretty unusual because he makes up rhymes all the time.*

2 Take out the puppet and have him introduce himself. *Hello, I'm a mellow rhyming fellow! Sir Rhymes-a-Lot is here to spread some rhyming cheer! What is your name?*

3 Ask one child to introduce her- or himself to Sir Rhymes-a-Lot. When the child says his or her name, have Sir Rhymes-a-Lot rhyme it: *Hello Nora, Flora, Cora, Bora. How do you rhyme today? Can you think of another word that rhymes with your name?*

4 Invite others in the class to help the child think of rhyming words (nonsense words included). Record them on chart paper if desired.

5 Ask that child to introduce a friend and play the game again. *Well, Nora, Flora, Cora, Bora, Tora, Zora, you have a wonderful long rhyming name. Oh my, oh gee, now who can you introduce to me?* That child then introduces someone else to Sir Rhymes-a-Lot, and the game continues until all children who want a turn have had one.

> **MATERIALS:** puppet, chart paper and markers (optional)
>
> **SKILLS:** auditory discrimination, listening, rhyming, vocabulary

Tips

- Make Sir Rhymes-a-Lot available throughout the day so that children can show him around the room. Use him to introduce snack time, a story, or a game. The more children hear his made-up rhymes, the more comfortable they will be making up their own.

- Use the puppet to excuse children from the circle. Have him say a silly rhyming word for their names, and see if they can guess who is being excused. *Sir Rhymes-a-Lot says, Muzie and Mally* (Suzie and Sally) *can go line up. What letter sound did I use?* (m)

Listen and Play

Rhythm instruments can provide an added dimension to listening skills. As children sing, they have to listen for when and how to play their instruments.

HOW-TO

1 Invite children to close their eyes, and have each child pull a rhythm instrument out of the bag. Say, *The instruments are feeling shy about coming out, so let's hug them close until we are ready to start.* This will keep things quiet until you begin singing.

2 Use a simple song to a familiar tune to practice listening for directions:

Make Sounds Softly
(Tune: "Are You Sleeping")

Make sounds softly, (2x)
Listen to me,
Listen to me,
Play them very loudly, (2x)
Just like me. (2x)

3 Invite children to suggest other types of sounds they can make with the instruments ("Make sounds happy" or "Play them very shyly"), and use them in the song. Each new verse will invite children to listen and match the sound to the words.

> **MATERIALS:** rhythm instruments in a pillowcase or large bag
>
> **SKILLS:** listening, speaking, singing, vocabulary, rhyming, creative expression

● Try the old favorite "Do You Know the Muffin Man?" to practice listening skills. Change the words to *Do You Know the Music Man?* and, in each verse, have children listen for which instrument is supposed to play. Then the drum (or other instrument) players do a solo.

Do you know the music man,
The music man, the music man,
Do you know the music man,
Who played drums right now?

I Spy Sounds

Understanding that each letter has a corresponding sound is an essential step in becoming a successful reader and writer. Build this awareness with a simple guessing game!

MATERIALS: small objects such as a rock, pen, book, and key

SKILLS: letter and letter-sound recognition, word recognition, listening, observation, fine-motor coordination

HOW-TO

1. Display four or five objects in the center of the circle and say the name of each object together. For instance: *rock, pen, book, key.*

2. Explain that you are going to play an I Spy game. *I spy with my little eye something that starts with P-P-P. What is it?* Invite a child to pick up the pen.

3. Now expand the game to the rest of the classroom. *I spy with my little eye something that is over in the library corner that starts with the same P-P-P sound* (a pillow).

4. Move to the next object in the circle and repeat. Start with something in the circle, then move on to things around the room.

5. You can increase the challenge by asking children to find new objects and having them lead the game.

Tips

⦿ By slowly expanding the field, you take children from the concrete experience to greater and wider levels of experience.

⦿ If children are having difficulty, add clues. For example, *I spy with my little eye something on the floor that starts with P-P-P. You can write with it.* (pencil)

Silly Syllables

Young children are naturals at playing with sounds!
The skill of knowing how to break a word into syllables
assists children in the process of decoding long words.

MATERIALS: chart paper, markers

SKILLS: auditory discrimination, phonemic awareness, vocabulary

HOW-TO

1 Explain that a syllable is part of a word and that some words have one syllable and others have more. Introduce the concept by saying a child's name and clapping the syllables in it. Repeat with a few children's names. Model and have children repeat each name.

2 Introduce a long word like *pineapple*. Say the word slowly and ask children to clap it with you. *Now I am going to say the first parts of the word and you fill in the last part. Ready? Pine, app…* (children say *lll*). Try several different long words that are familiar to children. They will have to listen carefully to be able to finish each word.

3 Time to get ever sillier! Take a long word like *rhinoceros* and invite children to change the last syllable to make up a silly new word. Record their words on chart paper. *Rhin-oc-er-goo! What do you think a rhinocergoo looks like?*

Tips

- Try this with all different words throughout the year.

- Provide art materials for children to draw some of their new word creations, and help them label them.

Sign 'n' Sing Attendance

Attendance can be a literacy-rich experience for children. In this activity, children write their names every day and sing them, too!

HOW-TO

1 Display chart paper near the circle time area. Write "Sign In" at the top. As children come to the circle, have them sign their name anywhere on the page with marker or crayon. You might introduce the activity by doing it yourself. *I am going to sign in to circle time by writing my name on this sheet. I start all the way on the left and write the letters to the right.* (Depending on children's age and level, you can write names in pencil and have them trace the letters over with marker.)

2 When everyone has signed in, say, *Let's see who is here today by singing a song:*

Who's in School?
(Tune: "Frère Jacques")

Who's in school?
Who's in school?
Read the names,
Read the names.
[child's name] is in school,
[child's name] is in school,
Welcome [child's name],
Welcome [child's name].

3 As children sing the song, the child whose name is sung stands up. At the end of the song, ask, *Who is missing today?*

MATERIALS: chart paper, markers or crayons

SKILLS: name recognition, fine-motor coordination, left-to-right progression, singing

- At the beginning of the year, children may scribble and draw their name. Celebrate all attempts at writing!

- If the area gets too crowded, children can sign in as they arrive in the morning or any time before circle time starts.

Lots of Labels

Instead of labeling the room for children, invite them to help you do it!
Soon you may find everything in your room labeled...even you!

HOW-TO

1 Introduce the activity by "playing forgetful"! You might say, *I have a problem that I hope you can help me with. You see, I just keep forgetting what things in our room are called. So I thought you could help me make labels for these things to help me remember. Can you help me?*

2 Point to a familiar object and ask children to name it for you. *Now this thing that we read has a name. Can you tell me what it is?* Children call out *book*!

3 Enlist children's help in making the label on an index card. *I want to write the word* book. *What letter do you think it starts with? Let's listen to the word again. Book. Yes,* B. *Book starts with a* B.

4 Write the word slowly on an index card. Show children how you start at the left side of the card and write toward the right. Say the word together, and tape it in place onto a book.

5 Next, point to something else in the area you want to label. *This flat thing here we are all sitting on, I know it starts with* R, *but I can't remember the rest. Can you help me make a label for this item? What is it? Rug!* Invite children to help you spell the word *rug* as you write it on the card.

6 Continue with several more items in sight of the circle time area. Invite children to suggest things to label. Repeat during the week until the room has lots of labels!

MATERIALS: index cards, markers and crayons, masking or clear packing tape

SKILLS: print awareness, writing, labeling, word recognition, left-to-right progression

Put out index cards in the writing area for children to make their own labels. Toward the end of the year, replace the teacher-made classroom labels with those children write themselves!

Introducing Journal Writing

One of the most effective ways for children to learn the process of journal writing is to watch it unfold in front of them! Model a journal entry so children can soon begin using their personal journals.

HOW-TO

1 Explain that keeping a journal is a way to record the special things that happen each day. Think of an event that happened recently in the class (such as a trip or a party). Tell children about your experience of it.

2 Now ask, *What shall I write? Where should I write the words? Which side of the paper should I start on?* Keep your writing simple, and say the words as you write. You can draw a simple picture to match your text.

3 As you go, point out punctuation. *I am going to put a period at the end of the sentence because I am finished with that thought. But this sentence says something exciting, so I am going to put a dot and a line above to make an exclamation point!*

4 Reread the journal entry together. Pass out children's journals for them to take to the tables and begin drawing and writing their own entries.

MATERIALS: chart paper, markers, blank children's journals

SKILLS: journal writing, print awareness, sequencing, creative expression

 Tips

◉ Remember that you are modeling art as well as writing. Draw freely! If you degrade your drawing or make apologies for it, children will begin to feel there is a "right" way to draw. Employ the same supportive techniques for your own drawing as your would for theirs!

◉ Periodically model adding a new entry to your journal. This way you can show different types of entries, such as special events, favorite things, or even a class event.

I Wrote a Letter...

Introduce children to the art and joy of letter writing by sharing your excitement over receiving a letter, and by modeling your reply.

MATERIALS: sample letter, chart paper, markers

SKILLS: letter writing, expressive language, vocabulary, handwriting

HOW-TO

1. With great excitement, show children the letter you brought to share with them. Point out the stamp and the address on the envelope. Ask, *Have you ever received a letter? Who was it from?* Tell children who yours is from, and read it aloud.

2. Ask children to help you write a letter in reply. Starting at the upper-left corner of a sheet of chart paper, demonstrate how to begin the letter. You might ask, *How did my letter from my sister start? What should I write first?*

3. Introduce words such as *To* and *Dear* by writing them down. Explain that these words are used to start a letter or note.

4. Time to write the letter! Invite children to suggest what you can say in your reply.

5. End by using the words *From* or *Love* as you close the letter, and read it back to children.

Tips

- At the writing center, put out a collection of envelopes and stationery to inspire letter writing. Provide stickers to use as stamps.

- Make a "post office" in the classroom (with a mailbox for each child), where children can send letters to their classmates!

Shopping Trip

List making is a form of writing that children can learn quickly, and it's a great way to learn new vocabulary.

> **MATERIALS:** grocery store circulars (newspaper inserts), sample shopping list, chart paper, markers
>
> **SKILLS:** expository writing, vocabulary, handwriting

HOW-TO

1 Talk about grocery shopping. *Do you go to the supermarket with your family? Does someone make a list of the things you need before you go?*

2 Show an example of a shopping list. Ask children to try to read the words on your list. Ask, *What do I need to get at the store?*

3 Introduce the grocery circulars and have children look through them. *Let's pretend we are going to the store to buy food for dinner. What should we get?*

4 As children suggest foods, record the items on chart paper. Encourage children to find the suggested food words in the circular and tell you how to spell and write them.

Tips

◉ Put out grocery circulars, pads and pencils, scissors, and glue sticks for children to make their own picture-word grocery lists at the writing center.

◉ Make lists by categories or aisles, such as dairy, meat, and produce.

◉ Set up a grocery store in the dramatic play area so that children can use their lists! Be sure to have boxes or play foods representing many of the foods on the list. Invite children to make signs and prices for all the foods.

Let's Write a Recipe

A very practical use of reading is following a recipe. In this activity, children will be putting familiar recipes into their own words. The result is often very funny!

MATERIALS: recipe cards or cookbook, chart paper, markers

SKILLS: expository writing, sequencing, following directions, vocabulary

HOW-TO

1 Show a favorite cookbook or recipe card. Ask, *Do you ever help cook at home? Does someone in your family use a recipe? What is a recipe?*

2 Choose a favorite familiar food that children are likely to know how to make, such as a peanut butter and jelly sandwich. Ask children to tell you how to make it. Write down their recipe ideas on chart paper, using the same format as a regular recipe (starting with an ingredient list and listing steps). When it is finished, read the recipe together.

3 Follow up with a cooking activity in which children need to follow a recipe. Ask them to point out the ingredients list, step 1, step 2, and so on.

Tips

- Set up a pretend cooking area in the dramatic play area. Provide play foods, dishes, and utensils.

- Place blank recipe cards in the writing center so that children can write their own.

What's It For?

Young children can more easily speculate if the subject is something they can see and even touch. An unusual object or prop can be a great way to start a "wonderment session" together.

MATERIALS: familiar objects that could have many different uses (such as string, tape, sheet or blanket, pencil, or notebook), chart paper, and markers

SKILLS: listening, observing, expressive language, creative expression

HOW-TO

1. Show a familiar object (like a piece of string) and invite children to consider different ways in which to use it. Uses may be familiar or unusual, such as making a necklace, hanging a mobile, tying a knot, tying it around your finger to remember something, or using as a headband!

2. Make a list on chart paper of children's ideas. Encourage them to think of silly ways to use the object (to make pretend spaghetti, as a shoelace, and so on).

Tips

○ Children usually have much more creative ideas for this type of activity than adults do. Don't worry if you can't think of many things to do with the object. They will probably help you!

◉ Eventually, use an unfamiliar object. An unusual tool, an instrument from a different culture or an uncommon fruit or vegetable can invite children to wonder. Ask, *What do you think this could be? How is it used?* Don't worry about getting the "right" answers. Relish the diversity of the ideas, and eventually tell children what you know about it.

What could we do with this blanket?
- roof for a fort
- sleep under it
- sit on it at the beach
- dress up like a ghost
- curl up and get warm
- magic carpet ride

Worth a Thousand Words

An interesting picture can spark thousands of words!
In this activity, children will ponder an interesting picture.

MATERIALS: interesting action photos or pictures from magazines and Web sites

SKILLS: listening, observing, expressive language, creative thinking and expression

HOW-TO

1 Show a picture and invite children to use their curiosity and creative thinking Ask, *What is happening now? What do you think might have happened just before this picture was taken? What might have started this situation?*

2 Ask, *What might happen next?* These types of questions invite children to organize their thinking within a time sequence and develop temporal understanding as well as prediction skills.

3 Invite children to draw pictures of their "before" and "after" ideas. Hang these in a time line in the circle time area so that children can read the story in pictures. Encourage them to use words like *first, next, last, then,* and *finally.*

Tips

⊙ Children may enjoy adding more and more to the picture time line. They might add another "before" event and another "after" event. Ask, *What do you think happened before that? What do you think happened after that?*

⊙ Share Tana Hoban's *Look Book* (Greenwillow, 1997), and examine the fascinating photographs within.

That's a Different Story

Familiar stories are an excellent starting place for questions that invite children to consider different viewpoints. Children will be exploring story structure and sequence at the same time.

MATERIALS: familiar folktales, fairy tales and books; chart paper, markers, art materials
Optional: flannel board and felt pieces for storytelling

SKILLS: listening, observing, expressive language, creative expression

HOW-TO

1 Read aloud a favorite fairy tale such as The Three Little Pigs. Since most children already know the story, you can invite them to tell it along with you. Use pictures from a book as a starting place or have them tell the story using felt pieces on the board.

2 After you've finished retelling the story, ask questions to get children thinking: *If you were one of the three pigs, what would you be thinking when the wolf was trying to get in your house? What if you were the wolf? How would you feel if you could never get in?*

3 Encourage children to consider the viewpoint of each of the characters. Together, brainstorm a list of feeling words that can be used in these discussions about stories. To help children read the words, draw a little face to go with each emotion.

Tips

- Continue the exploration of emotions and feelings in the art center. Provide materials for children to draw *angry*, paint *frightened*, sculpt *happy*!

- You can also use a familiar character like Clifford the Big Red Dog to inspire questioning. *What if Clifford suddenly became three inches tall? How would his stories be different?*

- Share *The True Story of the Three Little Pigs*, by Jon Scieszka (Puffin, 1997).

50

Word Wondering

As you play with language, young children become increasingly curious about words and writing. Use their curiosity to inspire some great circle time discussions filled with insightful questions and creative answers!

HOW-TO

1 On chart paper, write a simple word such as "pop." Ask, *What will happen to the word if we change the first letter? How many words can we create?*

2 Invite children to suggest letters (they can follow the alphabet frieze for help), and then listen for the real and pretend words they create. Point out that there is an important difference between real and nonsense words—nonsense words don't have any meaning!

3 Invite children to try out different sounds. *What sound does the T make? What does the word sound like when you put the T with the OP?*

4 Accept all suggestions equally. Children can even create their own meanings for nonsense words. *What could a "DOP" be?*

5 Put it all together into a song! Change the words to "POP Goes the Weasel" to fit the new spellings. Sing and move to the original song and then add the new words, asking, *What would the monkey do if "GOP" goes the weasel?* Use as many of their words as they can think of!

POP Goes the Weasel
Round and round the mulberry bush,
The Monkey chased the weasel.
The monkey laughed to see such a sight,
GOP goes the weasel!

> **MATERIALS:** chart paper, markers, alphabet chart or frieze
>
> **SKILLS:** listening, vocabulary, phonemic awareness, expressive language, creative expression

Tips

○ Keep a tally of the number of real and pretend words children create.

○ At another circle time, introduce the word *bug* or *pan* and ask children to suggest all the words they can create by changing the first letter of each word.

○ Introduce the many words for *Mom*. Ask, *How can we say* Mom *in other languages?* Write these in a row so that children can compare the different words (*madre* in Spanish, *mere* in French, *mitera* in Greek, *ima* in Hebrew, and so on). *What do you notice about the words for* Mom? (many start with the /m/ sound!)

Musical Wondering

If you can wonder about stories and things, why not songs?
By asking children to change the words to a song,
you build important language and listening skills.

HOW-TO

1 Choose a well-known song such as "The Bear Went Over the Mountain" to invite children to wonder about and consider different viewpoints. Sing the song the familiar way first.

The bear went over the mountain, (3X)
To see what he could see. (3X)
The bear went over the mountain to see what he could see!
He saw another mountain, (3X)
That's what he could see!

2 Ask children to suggest other things a bear might see going over the mountain, and add them to the next verses. They might pretend to move around the circle like bears to get the feel for his perspective.

3 Now ask, *What if an ant went over the mountain? What would it see? How would the ant's view be different from the bear's?* If children need help getting into the perspective, invite them to move around the circle like ants!

4 Sing the song again, substituting children's ideas. For instance:

The ant went over the mountain, (3X)
To see what he could see. (3X)
The ant went over the mountain to see what he could see!
He saw a giant red flower, (3X)
That's what he could see!

MATERIALS: none

SKILLS: listening, singing, vocabulary, expressive language

Tips

◉ Try suggesting other animals or locations for the song. *What would a hawk see? Where would a whale go and what would it see?*

◉ Other great songs to use are "I Know an Old Lady Who Swallowed a Fly" and "Farmer in the Dell."

What Would Happen If...

Young children can often handle abstract questions when presented appropriately. "What would happen if..." questions can be used to arouse children's curiosity about an idea—and invite their imagination to run wild!

HOW-TO

1 Introduce an open-ended question for children to ponder. Present a *"What would happen if..."* question, such as:

What would happen if fish walked and birds swam?
What would happen if the dinosaurs came back?
What would happen if grass was blue and the sky green?
What would happen if people always walked backward?
What would happen if there were no telephones?
What would happen if it rained food for breakfast?

2 Remind children that there are no right or wrong answers—only what they think! Write children's answers on chart paper.

3 Invite more children to suggest answers. Read all the answers to celebrate some great creative thinking!

> **MATERIALS:** chart paper, markers, other art and writing materials
>
> **SKILLS:** listening, expressive language

Tips

- At activity time, have children illustrate or write their ideas in the art or writing center.

- Let children make up their own questions and pose them to the group.

- Share *If Dinosaurs Came Back*, by Bernard Most (Voyager, 1984).

Scent Sense

Research shows that children gain more information about new experiences and topics when they explore through multisensory activities.

HOW-TO

1 In advance, put a different scent in each film container. Pass the containers around the circle and ask children to close their eyes, smell, and guess what is in each. Invite children to use words to describe the smell. For instance, if the scent is vanilla, words might be *sweet*, *yummy*, *gentle*, and so on.

2 Reveal the contents of the film canisters and check them against children's suggestions.

3 Now they are ready for some questions:

What does your sense of smell tell you about things?
Why do you think I asked you to close your eyes as you smelled?
What can you do with your sense of smell?
What is your favorite thing to smell? Why?

4 On chart paper, write the word "smell" at the center of a concept web, and record chidren's answers.

MATERIALS: plastic film containers, samples of different smells (cinnamon, pepper, cotton balls soaked with perfume, vinegar, or vanilla), chart paper, markers

SKILLS: vocabulary, descriptive language, expressive language

Tips

◉ Use props to introduce another sense. Use instruments or recorded sounds as you ask the questions: *How do you use your sense of hearing? What do sounds tell you? What is the best sound to hear? Is it an indoor sound? An outdoor sound?*

◉ Repeat the same activity, but focus on the sense of touch (put something tactile in a paper bag and pass it around).

Nature's Wonders

There are so many questions to ask about nature.
The following activity should get a great conversation started!
You can also make up your own questions using the same format.

MATERIALS: chart paper, markers, mural paper, watercolors or finger paints, music that in some way matches the weather

SKILLS: listening, expressive language, group discussion

HOW-TO

1 Choose questions about nature to spark children's thinking. Tie questions to the current weather. For instance, on a rainy day, ask:

What makes the rain?
Where does it come from?
Where does the water go after a rain?
What do the butterflies and bees do in the rain?
How do rainbows happen?
What is the best kind of rain?
What is the worst kind of rain?

2 Play some rainy day music, such as Handel's *Water Music* (or music that matches the mood of the current weather), and place a large sheet of mural paper inside the circle for children to paint a giant rainy day (or current weather) picture together!

Tips

◉ Remember, it is not important for children to get the "right" answer with these questions (this is more an exercise in creative thinking than fact gathering).

◉ Other topics and questions to wonder about include: snow, wind, sun, clouds, storms, rainbows, change of seasons, sudden changes in weather. Just look outside your window and wonder aloud!

The Alphabet Store

Children will be surprised to find the center of the circle filled with grocery store items! Once they start shopping, the fun with letters begins.

HOW-TO

1 Place the collection of grocery items in the center of your circle before children join the circle. Then call children to the circle with a song.

> **The Alphabet Store**
> (Tune: "The ABC Song")
>
> *ABCDEFG, come and shop the store with me.*
> *Can you find some foods to eat?*
> *Match the letters that you see!*
> *ABCDEFG, Came and shop the store with me!*

2 Choose children to hold the bags. Starting with *A*, ask children to read the letter and make its sound. Then ask, *Can you find foods that start with the same letter? Let's put them in [child's name]'s letter bag.* Hold up a food and ask children to say its name. Then have them put that food in the correct bag.

3 Repeat for each bag. At the end of the game, have each child who is holding a bag play "grocer" and say to the group, for instance, *I have the letter A and in my bag is an artichoke.* Then invite children to sing the Alphabet Store song with you!

MATERIALS: Pretend or real foods (or pictures of foods) that start with the letters *A* through *G* (such as apple, artichoke, banana, carrot, celery, cauliflower, doughnut, egg carton, eggplant, french fry container, grapes), 7 paper bags labeled with lower- and uppercase letters *A* through *G*.

SKILLS: letter recognition and matching, phonics, singing, group discussion, sequencing

Tips

• Place the grocery items in the dramatic play area for children to set up their own Alphabet Store. Provide paper and pencils for making shopping lists and grocery orders. Collect grocery store circulars for children to use.

• Using seven different letters of the alphabet, play the game again.

Musical Alphabet

Some children learn letters best through movement.
Use this game to help children recognize letters and their sounds.

HOW-TO

1 Choose five letter cards from the stack. Show each card and ask children to name the letter. To get things "moving," ask children to form the letter with their bodies. *How can you be a T? Can you get a partner to help you be an M?*

2 Tape the letters onto the floor in the shape of a circle in the circle time area (with enough elbow room around each).

3 Explain, *This game is like musical chairs, except instead of chairs you will move around letters as the music plays. When the music stops, find the letter that is called out and go to it.*

4 Put on the lively music and invite children to walk around the letters without touching them. Stop the music and call out a letter-related question, such as *Which letter begins all of these words: toast, tea, tomato?* Children then head toward the correct letter and gather around it. Congratulate everyone and go back to the dancing!

6 Put the music on again, then stop it and call out a different clue. At the end of the game collect all the letters and see if they spell anything (you can choose the letters to spell out certain words).

MATERIALS: large index cards with one uppercase letter printed on each (for classes with more than 26 children, repeat letters as needed), masking tape, lively music

SKILLS: letter recognition, phonemic awareness, listening

- This is a great game to play as a review of specific letters children are learning.

- Add a fun movement element to the game. When the music starts again, invite children to move in a way that starts with the target letter. For instance, tiptoe for *T*, or skip for *S*. Eventually children will head for the letter before you even call it out!

A, My Name Is...

Often the first letters children learn are the ones in their names. Here is a fun song and game to play with these familiar letters!

HOW-TO

1 Write the alphabet down the left side of a sheet of chart paper. Ask children to sing the traditional ABC song together as you point to the letters.

2 Explain that you have a new letter song to sing that uses the first letters of children's names!

3 Go through the alphabet chart and, for each letter, ask if there are any children in the class whose name starts with that letter. Write the name(s) next to each letter.

4 Complete the alphabet chart with children's names, and you are ready to sing. (For letters that have no corresponding names, ask children to think of other names that begin with that letter.)

> **A, My Name Is . . .**
> (Tune: "Down by the Station")
>
> A, my name is Amanda
> B, my name is Brian
> C, my name is Costanzo
> D, my name is Drew
> E, my name is Eli
> F, my name is Franz
> G, my name is Gene
> H, my name is Hope
> (And so on)
> ABCD, off we go!

MATERIALS: chart paper, markers

SKILLS: letter matching and recognition, singing, phonemic awareness, listening

Tips

⊙ Instead of having children make up names for the letters without corresponding names, have them clap the space in the song!

⊙ Leave the chart up in the circle time area so that children can sing the song on their own. Children may also like to write their name in their own handwriting.

⊙ Put out small squares of blank paper for children to illustrate the song chart with self-portraits, and attach them to the alphabet list.

58

ABC Charades

Here's a quick alphabet guessing game. Children will use letter recognition and kinesthetic skills as they sculpt their bodies or hands into each letter of the alphabet.

> **MATERIALS:** small plastic letters, letter blocks or letter cards, bag or box
>
> **SKILLS:** letter recognition, observation, following directions

HOW-TO

1. Explain that Charades is a game where one player pretends, without talking, to be something or someone while the group tries to guess. Say, *We are so good at the ABC's that we are going to use them to play Charades!*

2. Demonstrate a few letters for children to guess. For instance, demonstrate *X* by laying on the floor with your arms and legs spread out. Or make a *C* by curving your fingers and thumb into the letter shape.

3. Now it is their turn! Put the letters in a bag or box. Ask a child to choose a letter without showing it to anyone. Then he or she forms that letter using hands, fingers, and/or body, and the group tries to guess the letter.

4. If the group needs a clue, the child modeling the letter can say a word that starts with that letter.

 Tips

- This is a great game to play when you have a small amount of time to fill between activities or before dismissal time.

- Use this game as an informal assessment tool. You will see who has a strong command of the alphabet and who needs more letter practice.

Dance and Match

Here's a lively way to practice letter recognition skills. In this game, children dance and match upper- and lowercase letters.

HOW-TO

1 Start with a few different letter pairs. Show the uppercase letter cards and ask children to name the letters. Hand these to several children to hold up. Then show the lowercase letters and ask children to match them to the uppercase letters others are holding. Display the pairs in the center of the circle.

2 Gather the cards and shuffle them as you introduce the game. Explain, *Today we are going to put on music and play a letter match game. I am going to pass you a letter card. Without peeking, hold it against your body as you dance to the music. When the music stops, show your letter card and try to find someone with the matching letter. So if you have an uppercase D, find someone with a lowercase d.*

3 Play the music and let the game begin! Children dance and when the music stops, invite them to match their letters. When the letter pairs have found each other, ask them to say the sound of their letter. *Let's hear the D's. What does your letter say? Now let's hear it from the R's!* You might also ask children to think of a word that starts with their letter.

4 Next, have children pass back their letters. Reshuffle and have children choose a new card to dance with. Do several rounds so that children can find and say several different letters.

MATERIALS: rhythmic dance music, tape, sets of letter cards (one lowercase, one uppercase)

SKILLS: letter and letter-sound recognition, phonemic awareness, listening

Tips

● Play the game when you are introducing new letters and reviewing the rest.

● Make it more challenging by using commonly confused letters such as *d, b,* and *p* (only if children have already learned these letters in isolation).

Alphabet March

There is something about marching that young children love—
put on some great marching music and they're ready to go!
In this game, children "march around the alphabet."

HOW-TO

1 Invite children to help you tape alphabet cards in ABC order on the floor, forming a large circle. Sing the alphabet song as you work!

2 Play marching music and ask children to march around the circle to the beat of the music.

3 Stop the music and say, *Freeze!* Tell children to stop and look at the letter on which they are standing. Starting at the beginning of the alphabet, have them say aloud the letter names in order. (Say letters that do not have someone standing on them yourself.)

4 Remove a few letters and repeat. Remove several letters each round until only a few are left. As in musical chairs, children who do not have a letter to stand on leave the game and join the cheerleaders on the sidelines.

MATERIALS: large index cards with one uppercase letter printed on each, masking tape, lively marching music

SKILLS: letter recognition, phonemic awareness, listening

Tips

- Have children sing the alphabet song instead of using marching music.

- Have each child say his or her letter sound, or a word beginning with that sound, aloud.

ABC Cheer

Have you ever noticed how children get more involved in an activity when you use a fun prop? Children love to cheer with handmade megaphones!

HOW-TO

1 Ask children if they have ever seen cheerleaders at a sports game. *What do cheerleaders do? Do you know any cheers?* Invite children to share any cheers they know.

2 Introduce a new cheer. Explain that children will be saying the letters of the alphabet and one word that begins with each letter. (You might start the game using a classroom alphabet frieze that has pictures to go with each letter.)

3 At first, do a call and response cheer (you say the letter and they say a word). Write the alphabet and children's corresponding words on chart paper. (Eventually, have children reverse the roles—or even do the entire cheer themselves.)

The ABC Cheer

Give me a A. Apple!
Give me a B. Ball!
Give me a C. Cat!
Give me a D. Dog!
(and so on, through
  the alphabet)
What do you get?
The alphabet!

4 Now children are ready to create their megaphones. Ask, *Did you ever see someone use a megaphone to make his or her voice sound louder?* Give each child an empty paper towel tube to decorate with stickers and markers.

5 Demonstrate how to use the megaphone by talking without it, then talking into it. Ask, *How do I sound different? Let's use the megaphones as we say the ABC Cheer!*

> **MATERIALS:** chart paper, paper towel tubes (1 per child), stickers, markers, alphabet frieze (optional)
>
> **SKILLS:** letter recognition, phonemic awareness, creative thinking, vocabulary

- Children may like to add cheerleader motions too—they can make letter shapes with their bodies.

- Once children are familiar with the cheer using the words you've recorded on chart paper, invite them to think of different words for each of the letters. Make a new list.

Notes

Best-Ever Circle Time Activities: Language Building Scholastic Teaching Resources